Seymour Issac Hudgens

Exeter, Schooldays and Other Poems

Seymour Issac Hudgens

Exeter, Schooldays and Other Poems

ISBN/EAN: 9783744652483

Printed in Europe, USA, Canada, Australia, Japan

Cover: Foto ©Thomas Meinert / pixelio.de

More available books at **www.hansebooks.com**

PHILLIPS EXETER ACADEMY, EXETER, NEW HAMPSHIRE.
"*Long may ye stand, ye noble, beauteous walls.*"

(*Page 73.*)

EXETER,

SCHOOLDAYS

AND

OTHER POEMS

BY

SEYMOUR I. HUDGENS

Illustrated

CAMBRIDGE, MASS.
MOSES KING, PUBLISHER
HARVARD SQUARE

COPYRIGHT BY
SEYMOUR I. HUDGENS, CAMBRIDGE.
1882.

Franklin Press:
Stereotyped and Printed by
Rand, Avery, & Co.,
Boston.

TO HIS EXCELLENCY

CHARLES HENRY BELL, LL.D.

Governor of New Hampshire

THESE POEMS ARE INSCRIBED

BY THE AUTHOR

THE poems here collected, with the exception of two of the shorter ones, were written before coming to college.

CAMBRIDGE, *May, 1882.*

CONTENTS.

	PAGE
Exeter	11
Schooldays	43
A Vision	79
Edith	84
Loved Isle	88
Remembrance	90
A Reply	94
Mary	97
Crew Song	99
Gathering Fagots	101
My Love	103
Harvest Festival	105
My Angel sleeps	107
'Tis sweet	109
Longing	111
Epigram	113

EXETER.

Ah, happy hills! ah, pleasing shade!
Ah, fields beloved in vain!
Where once my careless childhood strayed,
A stranger yet to pain,
I feel the gales that from ye blow
A momentary bliss bestow,
As, waving fresh their gladsome wing,
My weary soul they seem to soothe,
And, redolent of joy and youth,
To breathe a second spring.

GRAY.

EXETER.

I WATCH the sea-fog as it westward floats,
   Spreading its ghostly sheet and wizard coats
O'er hill and dale; now sifting, falling through
The vaulted aisles of forests dark and blue;
Now hanging o'er, with winding-sheet, yon stream
That slowly moves, silvered by morning's beam.
To Stratham Hill it sweeps, and lingers on
Great Bay, and softly puts its fingers on
That beauteous landscape stretching to the sea.
Yon schooners lie in fast security;
The ponderous anchor slips the cat-head's hold,
And, plunging, seeks its bed in ocean's fold;
While loud and shrill the jarring cable rings.
The halyards freed, the falling block now sings

A song the seaman loves; the gallant ships
Are sleeping on old Ocean's azure lips.
No canvas flouts the slowly moving breeze;
No storm holds rule, the sailors are at ease;
No weird yet lovely music rises from
The harp-strings of the mast, by tempest's palm
Sublimely struck; the boatmen's roundelay,
How sharp and clear it strikes along the bay!
How distant woods and hills give back the song!
How clear it floats the verdant vale along!
The lightly dipping oar, the hoarse, dull tone
The rowlocks give, is music sweet alone.
But hark! the beating of the oar now nears
The strand, a huge, gigantic form appears;
The yawl, wrapt round by misty halo, rides
Upon the sandy beach, beneath the tides.
The followers of the watery deep step forth
Like fabled giants of the savage north.
The wondering swains in silence crowd around;
To each the other is a sight profound.

These gaze upon the genii of the deep,
While those a million rapturous wonders steep.

Now day in radiant splendor wakes to view;
The sea-mist settles as refreshing dew;
The hamlet near this hill's declining base
Is waking to the spring day's glad embrace;
The Isles of Shoals, in pearly, radiant light,
Give back its warm, rich glow, in splendor dight;
The shrouded Ocean sleeps his robe beneath;
Far eastward, with the blue sea as its sheath,
Boar's Head stands jutting in the azure wave;
Beyond, Cape Ann with dusk the east doth pave;
Dark Agamenticus a sentinel stands
Where days of yore saw signals [1] light the strand's
Indented, curving shore. From this high place
I see White Mountains gild the northern space.

[1] An allusion to watch-fires kept on the highest hills during the wars with England.

And, England, rememberest thou the fires among
These northern hills, their summits bold along?
Rememberest thou the gleams of fiercest light
That called from out their base, in freedom's night,
Volcanoes of the blasting flame that kept
With fiery wave thy haughty minions, swept
Thy hosts unto the ocean's barren shore?
That scorched thy insolence, to rise no more
On Freedom's continent, this northern shore?
The North, in sooth, forever shall be free,
And there the standards wave of liberty.
Oppression is a savage beast, that thrives
In southern climes, there grasps its victimed lives, —
The Israelite along the torrid Nile,
And Carthage, with its slowly wasting pile
Destroyed by Roman legions from the North,
Where Freedom's standard ever cometh forth;
The Tartar, scaling China's endless walls,
And proudly ruling in her emperor's halls;

The Huns in black destruction sweeping o'er
The Roman front, in fiercest clouds of war
Now issuing from, in tides, their northern home;
The Vandal and the Gaul o'ercoming Rome;
The childlike Aztec, in his torrid zone,
The haughty Spaniard rules on iron throne;
And Mexico's, the Inca's, idle gold,
Castilian sons did keep in fastest hold.

The sun is high, the breeze is fair, the bay,
Late pillowed on the strand, now dances gay,
And curling ripples o'er its bosom play.
Huzza! the yachts are out, the sails are set,
Their keels the dimpling surface gently fret,
And freshening winds and azure waves are met,
That late lay lulled in rest beneath their side.
How like a thing of life each boat doth ride!
How music sweet and curling waters meet!
How ride they onward down the purple bay!
How streaming pennants at their mast-heads play!

How part the waters 'neath their pointed bows!
What gentle furrows track these salt-sea ploughs!

But hark! what sounds are these that strike mine ear?
It is the far-off bells that quickly sear
With gloom my spirit, quaffing long and deep
At Nature's fount, where ne'er I fall asleep.
It is the academic bells that peal;
Those sweet yet melancholy notes, they steal
Along the river's valley, up the vales
They murmur, float from hill to hill, nor fails
Each note to stir the sluggish blood that flows
The dreamer's veins along. But speak, who knows,
Or thinks he knows, the idler's mind and heart.
To the same end are many ways; nor start,
Great mind, sublimely wise, if Nature's law
Transcends thy petty own, and mild doth draw
With silver chord her pupil to the goal.
For some 'twere better far for mind and soul

EXETER.

To closely follow devious plodding ways;
Of some, the panting soul that fires and sways
The mind and heart will balk or pine, nor drink
But where sage instinct points to wisdom's brink.

I seek for shaded walks, and turn my way
Toward the Eddy, where rippling waters play, —
Blessed spot, where sacred memories long will twine;
Blessed waters, flowing 'neath thy grove of pine;
Blessed stream, that whispers quiet to the ear;
Blessed river, winding, flowing, rolling here,
Where nought intrudes, and all we love's sincere.
In sadness' and in gladness' hour thy wave
Hast been a friend to me; and nothing, save
The effacing hand of Time, from memory's page
Shall tear thy mirrored form in life's pilgrimage.
Sweet Exeter, so gently flowing to
The sea 'mid woods and meads that seem to woo
'Thee to their fond embrace, and kiss thy wave;
Sweet Exeter, upon whose placid face
The fern-beds waft their breath, thy beauty grace,

Along whose bank the partridge drums his note,
Adown whose wave the rowboats idly float;
Sweet river, winding, rolling, to the sea,
Accept this pensive, idle song from me.
Four long, long years I've strolled along thy tide.
Adieu, loved stream! adieu, thou forest's bride!
Adieu, ye hoary pines that kiss the sky!
Adieu, ye monarch trees that wave on high!
Adieu, thou cool-lipped stream, with sparkling tide,
That slowly trickles to the river's side!
And here the schoolboys carve their letters bold,
And think, forsooth, 'twill live when they are old.
How deeply I have loved thy moonlight face,
Nor less thy sombre mien when clouds do chase
Grim shadows o'er thy placid, sleeping breast!
But most thou'rt dear to me when heaven is dressed
In diamond robes, when all below reflect
Those gems above, thy wave with stars bespecked.
'Tis then the whippoorwill attunes his lay;
'Tis then, when stars take on their brightest ray,
He wakes his song to sweetest melody.

These oaks, whose rugged branches lean them o'er,
And glass their forms upon the watery floor
That lies beneath their feet, fond sports have seen.
Ye old, storm-beaten oaks that deck the green
Below, and rear aloft your monarch heads
Unto the sky, whose base the student treads,
Ye noble forest trees now marked by Time's
Rough hand, repeat to us from different climes
The sportive bands that years, long years, ye've
    seen ;
Tell of the silver locks upon this green,
Perchance, that time has brought. Ah! would ye
    tell
The tale their wrinkled brows repeat? 'Tis well.
The Fates do kindly hide their dark decree.
Let youth light up with joy what ne'er may be,
And let the giddy thought dash gayly on,
And let the throbbing pulse run daily on;
Too soon the crimson current slacks its pace;
Too soon the fiery thought to age gives place.

In youth or age 'tis all the same, ye trees
That lean above the tide, ye greet the knees
That tottering seek your shade; ye wear a gown
As bright as when in youth they reached this
    town;
Ye give in echoes clear the music sweet
That rises from this moonlight deep, ye greet
With joy the homeward-floating skiff, ye list
The rowlock's moan above the river's mist;
The lightly dipping oar, perchance a white
Sail set, the dusky forms that many a night
Glide softly by, the oar at rest, — ye've seen,
Ye mighty monarchs, standing on this green.

Now, up from meadows sweet with May or June,
The bobolinks, on fluttering wings, attune
Their medley song, their sweetest, wildest lay;
The thicket-thrush salutes the waning day;
And in the distance robins warble forth
Their vesper-songs in gardens at the north.

The gnarled "Oaks" preferred by these, while those
Descend to "Stony Point," where gently flows
Piscataqua, declining to the sea.
The fisherman his craft with energy
There sculls, surcharged anew with finny spoil,
Now rows against the seaward tide with toil,
Now slowly beats his way against the breeze.
Yon schooner now is riding at her ease;
Her sails are closely furled, her voyage o'er,
The storm-tossed farers of the deep on shore.

'Tis eve: the sombre veil that shades the east
Is rising high. Not yet hath wholly ceased
The rule of waning day; but gently falls
The softening shade of night, as in these halls
Of death alone I tread; the whippoorwill
Has strung his nightly lyre, the soul to fill
With pensive song; the beetle's drowsy flight
Now fills the evening air; nor yet hath night
With sombre wing o'erspread this pensive scene;

Where all is quiet, peace, and life serene;—
On yonder hill the farmer's home is seen.
And here was borne the honored teacher, slow
And sadly, to his aged tomb; below
These whispering pines and elms he lies in rest,
Where nought of flesh or earth can more molest.
And slowly, slowly, tolled the old church-bell;
And sadly, sadly, rung his parting knell;
And sad and slow the mourners rustled by.

When wreaths upon the soldier's grave make fair
His lowly sleep, regale rich summer's air,
A tribute to two graves I humbly bear.
The teacher's sacred dust by taught is blessed,
His memory treasured, in the heart caressed,
When mossy tablets rest above his clay.
Not his to seek the Senate's praise: his day
Of glory, when his pupils tribute bring
To him who poised young Science' untrained
    wing,

Brought down the heavenly flame, made straight the
  way,
Sent forth disciples into new-born day.
And here distinction's mark hath ceased: the high,
The low, in common dust together lie.
Man's titles and his power — what are they now?
Ambition, wealth, are levelled by death's plough.
Beneath one grassy turf alike they sleep,
And now the drooping willows o'er them weep.
Sweet evening's golden gems are in the sky,
The distant pines resound the night-bird's cry.
Now fades yon rural landscape into night,
And sombre darkness' wing shuts out the sight:
In pensive mood, and slow advancing tread,
I leave for aye this city of the dead.

'Tis eve, and swelling strains of music greet
The lonely wanderer on the quiet street.
Those outdoor vespers to the dying day,
The merry schoolboy's joyous vocal lay;

The flute is heard upon the evening air, —
The mellow, low-voiced flute, the schoolboy's care.
The pale-faced student bends above his task,
Or fills with midnight oil his failing flask, —
Attempts deep learning's mystery to unmask.

The scene is changed: I hear the hounds that bay
Upon the scent, deep-mouthed, this leaden day;
The lately-fallen snow, the hunter's glee,
Gives ecstasy to him, delight to me.
I view a valley's long, majestic sweep,
And, draining this, a mighty river deep,
Skirted along with lofty, various wood,
Where oft I've roamed in melancholy mood,
When autumn winds a pensive spirit wooed;
Where summer verdure wears her richest green,
And streamlets flow the skirting woods between;
Where autumn wears her long, long, dreamy dress,
And Indian summer smiles in loveliness;

Where clustering vineyards clothe the southern hills,
Protected from the winter's blighting chills;
Where Dionysus might again be king,
Teach all the heavy load of grief to fling,
And harmless revel, song, and joy to keep;
Where boundless flowering meadows rise and fall,
Now calm, now wildly tossed by summer squall.

But hark! Far down the river's sweeping course
They come, — the hounds, the men, and swiftest horse;
They sweep along its margin, seek each trend;
Now here, now there, their eager course they bend.
They have their prey, — the savage wolf or fox, —
Nor longer will he feed upon their flocks.
They near a broad estate, where ample cheer
From larger heart and board is always near.
They feast themselves, the horse, and well-spent hounds;
The rustic bowl then freely goes the rounds,

And jolly spirits, joke, and comic tale,
Employ the huntsmen erewhile from the vale.
How oft, when deepest gloom and sorrow's dart
My bitter portion seemed, unto thy heart
I've fled for sympathy, a true man's cheer,
And oft have known in thee a feeling tear!
A more than parent often thou hast been,
Extended sympathy thy home within.
A mind of genius' mould, a mighty soul,
Had ample learning been thy lot, — a roll
Enduring on the stage of life, thou'dst made;
And since in need you aided me, and stayed
My faltering hand, my heart doth call the flight
Of fancy wandering from her visions bright.

The tower-clocks ring out their wintry song,
That waves and swells in echoes sweet and long;
They beat pulsations every passing hour,
That wake the country round with solemn power;

They mark the ever onward pace of time,
And beat the distant pines in measured chime;
They are the throbs that mark, that slowly beat,
The farmer's life, the swain's retirement sweet,
Good cheer and health and rest the farmer's lot
Where peace and plenty reign, — his toils forgot.
His golden store of maize; his mows that groan
With loaded hay, his meadows' yearly loan;
His winter's store of autumn fodder bright;
His cider-mug, that cheers the wintry night;
His varied store his hardy orchards yield;
His rooty products from the autumn field;
His stanchels long, where well-kept cattle feed;
His woolly fold, safe from the prowler's greed;
His well-filled dairy, winter's bounteous store;
His glowing fireplace, never asking more;
His balanced books; freedom from every care;
His self-complacent, independent air, —
These are the farmer's own well-earned delights,
That give contentment to his wintry nights.

'Tis morn: this ancient town is clad in white,
Fair offspring from the sombre womb of night:
Like a fair bride upon her wedding-day,
She stands in fleecy robes bedecked, so gay.
But ho! the sun is rolling from the pines:
He gilds their snowy crests with golden lines,
And casts a flood of light upon this scene.
Fantastic stand the aged elms: between
Them plod, perchance, the country team adown
The snowy vista's length. This wintry town
Fantastic stands, with arching, vaulted streets;
In bridal dress the waking day she greets.
A thousand hearths are waking into life,
A thousand homes begin existent strife:
The sturdy townsmen, muffled close and warm,
File out to clear away the mighty storm.

And yonder lie the borough's slumbering dead,
Enrobed beneath their silent, snowy bed;

Though all is still, yet flaps my country's trust
Gently and slow above the soldier's dust;
Her banner's faded shreds there guard his sleep,
As through the sombre pines the chill winds creep.
Thou emblem of the free, 'tis meet to wave
Above the dead, who, living, fearless gave
Their all, their lives, our country's life to save;
Their fittest requiem be thy rustling folds
Above where now the soldier's body moulds.
And may thou wave, thou banner of the free,
O'er this great land, and o'er surrounding sea;
Fling wide and free thy beauteous waving form,
Float on the gentle breeze and in the storm.

'Tis winter's night; and learning's halls are clad
On high with snowy robes of light, that had
Till late their autumn garb: their gilded vane
Casts back the moon's full light o'er many a pane.
'Tis cold: but merrily now ring the bells;
And on the silver air their music swells,

And to the spangled sky they wildly ring,
And to the startled night their voices fling.
The distant pines give back their sweet refrain,
That dances o'er the whitened meadow's plain.
'Tis cold; yet youth's young blood is throbbing high,
And asks but sport to quench his passions dry.
The mettled barb is brought, all nerved for speed:
Away, away, they fly, the youth and steed;
The landscape swims before his dizzy sight
As on and on he flies into the night.
And there and then was sweetened youthful joy,
And there and then the charms of being a boy.
O youth! can Time e'er change thy rosy hour?
Will ever storms of darkness o'er thee lower?
Laugh on, nor know too soon the woes of life;
Laugh on, nor dwell upon the coming strife.

Once more on Stratham's wind-swept crest I stand,
Once more these wooded vales to view expand.

The scene, 'tis moonlight now (for this more sweet) ;
Before 'twas daylight's scene : a friend did greet
Each kindly impulse springing from the scene.
'Tis four long years, long years, that intervene.
'Tis moonlight on the waters bright; each star
Upon the deep is imaged from afar ;
The dews, like holy incense fill the air ;
Each blade and leaf is gemmed with crystals rare ;
And music sweet is on the moonlight deep.
The rowboat's slow advancing, measured sweep
Resounds the rowlock's following, hoarse reply ;
The pale-faced stars have lightly kissed the wave ;
The swelling tides the shores declining lave ;
The ploughman's plodding task is done, and o'er
His wearied frame sweet slumber rests once more.
His oxen, erewhile shambling from the field,
No longer 'neath their massive yoke are steeled,
But, freed from bondage 'fore the stubborn share,
Now graze, or rest, beneath the evening air.
The cock's shrill note is hushed ; beneath his care,

His feathered brood is lulled to deepest rest,
And tinkling folds the welcome earth have pressed.
The latest, lagging wain, from upland wood,
Perchance, now homeward threads the weary road:
The hamlet's spire is bathed in deepest light,
Its angel-vane now stands the guard of night.

There is a beauteous form to whom I would
A verse or two indite; and if she should
Adjudge them rough, uncouth, or very bold,
I pray her paint the heart-strings that of old
Did throb, adjusted to the sweetest note,
O'erstrained by time, or chilled by fortune's vote.

 Maiden, with those lashes dark,
  'Neath which passion's fire doth flood,
 Often, idly in my bark,
  I have glided through thy wood.

But no more thy stream I know;
   Squamscot's bank's a memory;
And thy smile of long ago —
   Will it smile again on me?

And no more thy woods I roam,
   Wrapt in nature's deepest thought;
And no more I see thy home
   With thine angel presence fraught.

Can I say those saddest words?
   Can I say, Adieu, adieu,
When thy spirit's presence girds,
   Lifts my hope again to you?

   Long I've felt thy curfew bell
   And thy funeral knell
   Work their magic on my soul
   By their solemn toll;

And thy happy wedding voice
At the bridegroom's choice,
And the old year's heavy tone
In its dying groan;

And the New Year's merry ring
On the night air fling
Music full of hope, and trust
In a God who's just.

But to-night thou'lt chant for me
Saddest melody;
Ring to night, thy farewell roll;
Aged watchman, toll.

The curfew slowly tolls the dying day,[1]
All toil hath ceased; the latest twilight ray

---

[1] Gray's line will at once be seen in this. Coins with the stamp of rulers and kings on them live when history is no more. A thought that has Gray's stamp on it can never be recast. It can only be borrowed.

Has fled; the lamps are out, the hearths are cold;
Sweet slumber keeps this town in fastest hold,
And fans with downy wing the young and old.
Sleep, infant, pillowed on thy mother's breast;
Sleep, youth, by parents' care endeared, caressed;
Sleep, maid, with angel's beauty in thy face;
Sleep, bride, with hope that does thy beauty grace;
Sleep, mother, troubled for a wayward son;
Sleep, father, ere thy daily toil's begun;
Sleep, silvered age, thy race will soon be run.
The poor forget their toil in slumber's hour,
Nor know they now the woes of mammon's power.
It gives us strength, it lights again the eye,
Divides the past, — worn-out, and sped for aye, —
And wakes the morrow, bright with new-born hope;
It gives us strength to-day, that we may cope
With life's reality; in visions sweet,
It gilds the morrow; it is our retreat
From care and woe; by dream's prophetic eye
We catch sweet glimpses of futurity;

In dreams the past oft sweetest re-appears,
And, time forgot, we're young in silvered years.

'Tis night, and quiet holds this ancient town:
The fading twilight's fled; and night, with gown
Of darksome hue, enshrouds each living thing.
'Tis night, and stillness rests on eagle wing
Above all things; the azure vault with stars
Is set; the Milky Way expands its bars,
With mystic beauty spread; the winds are hushed;
The bay, late dimpling 'neath the sun's full-flushed
And molten disk, with shining gems is set;
The mist that soars above the falls doth fret
All mortal skill to paint, like incense sweet
It rises to the sky on downy feet;
The rippling waves are pillowed in sweet rest.

'Tis done; and o'er this scene I love to dwell:
These memories dear no tongue nor pen can tell;
Deep in the heart's recess they nestle close,
And nought but time their sweetness may disclose.

These scenes, endeared on Memory's sacred shrine;
These years — how fleeting, yet how long — that
    twine
Their mystic tendrils in the schoolboy's heart, —
Alas! are sped: from classic scenes I part.
All, all, is o'er; and ere the chord has broke,
That fondly, dearly, binds me to this scene,
A lingering farewell of this view serene
I take: soon manhood's cares will intervene.

    Adieu, ye elms that wave on high!
      Adieu, ye shaded walks below!
    Adieu, thou stream that flows close by!
      Adieu, old town, before I go!

    Adieu, ye neighboring hills around!
      Adieu, ye woods of sombre hue!
    Adieu, the ocean's moaning sound!
      Ye vales that charm the eye, adieu!

SCHOOLDAYS.

> *Cur apricum*
> *Oderit campum, patiens pulveris atque solis?*
> *Cur timet flavum Tiberim tangere? Cur olivum*
> *Sanguine viperino*
> *Cautius vitat, neque jam livida gestat armis*
> *Brachia, sæpe disco,*
> *Sæpe trans finem jaculo nobilis expedito?*
>
> HORACE.

Say, Father Thames, for thou hast seen
Full many a sprightly race,
Disporting on thy margent green,
The paths of pleasure trace,
Who foremost now delight to cleave
With pliant arm thy glassy wave?
The captive linnet which inthrall?
What idle progeny succeed
To chase the rolling circle's speed,
Or urge the flying ball?

GRAY.

GORHAM HALL AND ABBOT HALL.
Phillips Exeter Academy.

"*Long may old Time look kindly on these halls!*" (*page 73.*)

SCHOOLDAYS.

SLOW tolls the bell within yon classic spire;
    The boys are tripping o'er, in neat attire,
The green in front, the place for tennis strife.
This quaint old town awakes with youth's new life;
And fevered, stirring scenes disturb her sleep.
But who can paint in colors true, nor weep,
Who knows the pangs that rend the schoolboy's soul?
What seas of memory o'er his mind doth roll!
What scenes of childhood's hour for aye are flown!
What bitter tears are his to share alone!
What thoughts of home, sweet home, he has no more!
What sister knows, except on dreamland's shore!

What mother smiles upon his daily woes! —
This youthful exile, torn by many throes.

Give o'er, the troubled scenes of life awake;
A thousand burying troubles on him break;
Yet darker seems the youthful sea of life,
Yet darker still the uncertain scene of strife.
But ah! the dawn of waking thought is born,
The world is new beneath its radiant morn;
His gladsome soul leaps forth to new-born day,
And faces kind that greet, his fears allay.
Ay, true, a world is dawning on his mind, —
A world before, a home with prayers behind.
Young life beats high with hope of future fame;
Life's throbbing current in each tender frame
Is warm with joy, the world in splendor dressed.

The robust boy is here, — warm heart, strong brain;
His mind he speaks, and hardly wears the chain;

SCHOOLDAYS. 45

Youth's ruddy wave is dashing high along
His veins, — clear eye, with feelings deep and strong.
Robust schoolboy, my heart most leans to thee:
Thy ways most touch its chords of sympathy.
And see the spare, pale youth, whom Nature gave
With grudging hand: he's timid, shy, and grave;
His mind, of plastic mould, is easy wrought
Beneath the master's shaping hand of thought.
To guide the gently flowing stream, man's art
Sufficient is; but mountain torrents start
His utmost skill to check, control, or guide;
And dash they madly on unto the tide.
'Tis so in school: the gently flowing thought
Is led, in fashion's mould is easy wrought.
But wonder not, if Nature's thought rejects
Conventional rules, from beaten roads deflects.
The bright, unclouded mind of heavenly birth,
That seems not formed to dwell, but flee this earth;

The dull, unlighted mind; the fiery thought, —
All kinds and grades are here together brought:
In one scholastic course their race is run,
And in the lowest class their trials begun.

In looking down the scene of garnered time
That makes the schoolboy's life, if short, sublime
With thought and deed, what rivers of memory
Flow in, and whelm the soul, and damp the eye!
What triumphs, and defeated, airy schemes!
What floods of light upon the soul now streams!
What chilling shadows dark now hide these gleams!
What bright careers cut short, what severed ties,
What faces lost for aye to weeping eyes!
And here one face in grief I call to mind.
Dear Marcus, if thy shade is on the wind,
And if departed spirits hover o'er
Fond scenes and friends of earth, who cannot more
Embrace their fleshy forms upon this shore,
Give kindly ear unto the winds that waft
This song for thee, young victim of Death's shaft.

When autumn wore her golden veil,
    When flowers had ceased to bloom,
We raised for thee funereal wail,
    And bore thee to thy tomb.

In youth's full flush and hope thou passed
    From out our longing sight:
We mourned thee till chill autumn's blast
    Was lost in winter's night.

O Death! how bitter is thy sting
    In life's full flushing morn,
When youth soars high on gallant wing,
    The child of nature born!

How, then, thou pluck'st with ruthless hand
    The flower just kissing day,
And tak'st from youth's full, gladsome band
    Her brightest, worthiest ray.

Fit scenes, in sooth, are these, for genius' birth, —
Fit scenes, if ever such there be on earth,
To fashion forth the senatorial course;
These lifelike forms of those who've run the course,
Who've battled in our Congress' stately walls,
Or labored long in education's halls, —
Great Webster on my left, and Everett, Cass,
And Abbot on the right; nor lightly pass
The last revered and honored form, who here,
Prometheus-like, brought down, to bless and cheer,
The heavenly fire, and fashion genius' mould,
From the rude elements bring forth the gold.
Methinks this breathing group within each frame
Sweet converse hold; on him reflect the flame
Of living, truthful light their names inspire;
Revere that sacred form, their common sire.

Ay, ours is Freedom's cherished, sacred land:
No fettering shackles, clinched by kingly hand,

Here bind the mind's free scope, nor steal her wreath;
No James to dictate to our schools, or sheathe
Oppression's sword in creed's usurping sheath.
Yes, Athens, thy thought wast free; the world for aye
Will own thee learning's king: the immortal ray
That fires the mind must all be free, or wane.
Bear witness, Russia, Prussia, England, Spain,
Where learning's fed and nourished, granted all;
But let her strike at power, how quick her fall!

The boys are out, their recitations o'er.
No longer studious minds collect the lore
From many an ancient page, nor puzzle o'er
Deep mathematics' laws; wise history's page,
With all its golden lore for age on age,
Is thrown aside, and physics' material laws,
Cæsar and Tully, Xenophon, rhetoric's saws,
And Virgil's softly moving strain, the power
Sublime to paint man, nature, beast, or flower,

And Homer's godlike song, — all, all, forgot;
Along the green in many a clustering knot
The schoolboys speed: these seek the river's side.
Their shells are out, they rest upon the tide.
The bay with dimpling cheek now seems to woo
Them to its glad embrace. Huzza! the blue
Waves' crest is glad, with many a white sail set,
And eager crowds along the banks are met.
The swelling tide gives back in purple set
Each form along its shore, the wind is low;
Fond hearts are beating high. The boats below, —
They man the oars, now poised upon the tide
They rest, the signal-shot they eager bide.
'Tis off! they move, they fly along the waves' blue
    crest: —
Each crew, in turn, by lovers fond's caressed:
Now this, now that, by skilful toil prevails.
How bend they to their oars! nor one who quails
Beneath the sturdy strokes; how waters part
Before the boats' sharp bows! high beats each heart.

GIDEON L. SOULE.
Instructor for fifty years at Phillips Exeter Academy.

"And here was borne the honored teacher, slow
And sadly, to his aged tomb." (*page 22.*)

And now the foremost flies beyond the goal,
The flag-boat's bow is passed, and honor's role
Is proudly won. The air is rent with cheers.

Some swing in graceful curves upon the green
The racket; gently soars the ball between
The facing courts, and o'er the netting's guard.
Some play at quoits; croquet now some regard.
But pass we to the Campus, ever dear
With schoolboy memories thick clustered here.
A varied scene here greets the feasting eye, —
A gently sloping field whereon doth vie
In healthful sport full many a happy youth,
Surrounded half by woods of closest growth,
That renders back in echoes long and loud
The pealing shouts that leave the assembled crowd;
And half by gardens and the farmers' road.
On holidays, when freed from labor's goad,
Full oft we've swept in counter-charge this plain;
Full oft impelled with sturdy foot amain

The hogshide ball to either homeward goal;
Full oft in fleetest course have gained the pole,
And heard with pride our schoolmates' ready cheer.
Ah "Bravo!" from a classmate's lips, how dear!
'Tis won in equal strife: swift time will fade
The teacher's praise; but this with gold's inlaid,
And silvered age will fondly dote on praise
Bestowed for feats at play, when tutors' bays
Are faded in the past. These charge to reach
Their goal, and drive the ball in every breach
That opes throughout the opposing, struggling lines,
While those repel the charge by shrewd designs.
The ball is caught, and skilful feet impel
It through the air, and victory's hopes dispel.

Full oft I've been a truant, fled these walls
To keep communion with my soul's own eye,
To drink from Mother Nature's fount, to try
The steeps of history's lore, to peer far o'er

The desert of man's deeds, since Time her flight
Began, — a mighty waste, a mournful sight.
But hark! loud peals the bell from learning's dome,
And Science calls her youths within her home:
From Maine to Texas, o'er this mighty land,
From Minnesota in the shivering north,
To blooming Florida, her sons come forth;
Yea, e'en the golden Orient doth demand
Admittance to her sacred, holy walls;
The Western Indies too, within these halls
Have sought and found for thirsting lips the fount.
Glad welcome give for aye these youths, to mount
From out the bales of ignorance; ye walls,
Throw wide thy portals, freedom in thy halls,
And let the setting sun sweet tidings bear
To their own land, so dead, yet death so fair;
The new in life extend, to greet, thy hand,
The old in death beyond Pacific's strand.
Ye youths, go back, and in your Eastern clime
Rear high the templed halls of truth, that time

Shall kindly smile upon; drive back the cloud
Of ignorance that doth your land enshroud:
So shall unnumbered ages yet to be,
So shall unnumbered peoples you shall free
From brooding darkness' curse, thy names revere.

Here some haste to the green declining bank,
And flee their studious toil: they leave the plank,
And headlong plunge beneath the purple wave;
The schoolroom, teacher, Latin, Greek, all save
The watery sport, alike in each's forgot,
And healthful pastimes are their happy lot.
The dimpling current wooes them to its breast,
And here from tasking toil they seek their rest.
The watery element invites them now,
And buoyant limbs the billows lightly plough;
The waters lave their limbs; these nymphs the deep
Doth gladly own, doth fondly hold in keep, —
Now gently lulls them as inviting sleep,

Now rocks them on her azure, heaving breast,
Again she calms them into sweetest rest.
Oft we have cleft with buoyant limbs thy form,
Old oak; with heart full beating high and warm
We've cut with pliant limb thy foliage green,
That mirrored lies the wave and heavens between.

'Tis winter's night, and on the casement falls
The fleecy snow, and nought there is that calls
The studious, patient youth from learning's toils.
His page is set, his fireplace trimmed, his oil —
The midnight star that lights his weary way —
Now glimmers through the curtained close of day.
The schoolboy's care is o'er his labored page
Of classic lore and history, — the stage
Whereon all actors, since remotest time
Began, before us pass in view sublime.
The tower-clocks, with muffled, heavy toll,
Strike out the passing hour; the distant roll

Of Ocean breaking on his wintry shore
Now wanes, now swells, to one low, rumbling roar.
The street-lights glimmer through the falling snow,
And as the night wears on they shorter grow.
'Tis night; and all is o'er. In visions blessed,
The schoolboy's mind on fleetest wing again
Doth speed its homeward way, nor knows the pain,
The pang, that separation soon must bring.
His midnight lamp is out; and anger's sting,
Sarcasm's venomed tooth, what are they now?
If late he felt, sweet sleep doth calm his brow.

'Tis winter's night; but youth's young blood is warm,
And skilful feet in mazy toil the charm
Of ice-king try. With lightning speed they skim
The frozen wave in movements neat and trim.
With skates and crook in hand, these seek the "Cove,"
And healthful sport enjoy beneath the grove.

Some wend their way through woods of deepest
    pine,
And thread for miles the stream, nor aught repine;
Some sweep in mazy whirl broad Squamscot's face,
And gather here a fund of health and grace;
The neighboring hills are climbed with sled in hand,
And all jump on, — a merry, reckless band;
And these, by master's rare indulging grace,
Seek out (their joy) some neighboring country-
    place, —
Amesbury town, New England's poet's home;
Perchance to distant Haverhill they roam;
Old Kingston's plain they hie them quickly through,
And lofty Kensington repass anew;
While those to Boar's Head urge their steeds apace,
And gaze upon old Ocean's wintry face,
Or speed away to ancient Portsmouth town.

'Tis early autumn time: the winds sigh low
And sweet to woo the pensive thought; below,

The farms outspread in panoramic view, —
Here golden with the ripening ear, there blue
With winding, spreading stream: here deepest green
With second growth, a contrast to the scene;
There orchards bending with their ripening fruit,
That soon will feed the hungry cider-mill's shute:
Here neighboring pine-clad hills of sombre hue,
Or gorgeous, variegated woods, the view
Make up; there, 'mid the haze and halo, stand
Along the dreamy horizon the grand
Old northern hills I oft have trod upon.
This is the view outspread from Kensington;
But, Frank, in vain I try this scene to paint,
Where we how oft have stood, and heard the
    plaint
Of distant Ocean beating on his shore.
Ah! will we hear again his rumbling roar?
This joy we ne'er may have, ah, nevermore!
And like a girl I've loved thee, Frank: those lips
With boyish curl, where gentle frolic skips;

Those deep brown eyes — but who with pen or brush
Can paint the laugh, the tear, the passions' rush,
The deep and speechless gaze of fervent love
That burns in mortal caskets here — above
Doth tell a tale, unthread a puzzling maze,
Apply a balm to hearts that here, in days
Of flesh and blind mortality, did bleed?
The jealous, sidelong glance, the lustful deed
That spoke in leer, and love's sweet, stolen glance.
Forgive this rush of fancy's wild expanse.
Thy locks of waving auburn o'er a brow
Of girl-like beauty — still I see thee now
In pensive habit watching stately ships
That eastward glide along; — methinks those lips
With time may wear a sadder, graver mould.
Forbid! but may their gentle sadness' fold,
Be ever as it was in days now o'er,
When you and I did delve the classic lore!
You rapid progress made, and eager wrought,
And fed a clear-toned brain all formed for thought.

First trying, vying, in the schoolboy race,
Each daily task was met within the trace;
But soon arose a longing vague and still
And deep, impatience at the ripest skill,
A wish to trample forms beneath my feet;
Yet ever quick the welcome page to greet,
And walk with Nature and with Nature's man,
And converse keep, — attempt to con her plan.
'Twas this I own, — your constant, clear-brained toil
Robbed me, and gave to you scholastic spoil.
With early autumn leaves I twine thy brow,
A pallid, golden wreath I bring; for thou
Art pensive Autumn's thoughtful, beauteous child;
And like her gently sighing winds, that mild,
Sweet symphony around us nightly keep,
Is thy sweet spirit, tender, sad, and deep.

Some test enduring strength and fleetest speed;
They fly along the course like swiftest steed;

They test their skill and speed in hurdle-race;
They try united skill in three-legged pace;
They hurl with skilful arm far o'er the green
The ball; the tug of war each class between
Is fought; the mighty hammer those now throw,
And these in skilful walk now by us go;
The boat crews train the coming race to meet;
The boys now hie them by on nimble feet;
These run on tiptoes light, with easy grace,
And those in walk go on a longer space.
Some test enduring strength and swiftest feet
At "hare-and-hounds." They leave the winding street,
And speed them to the wood's secretest glen
Through devious winding ways. The hares, who ken
Each wily trick, swift lead the hounds; they seek
The wooded dell, the marsh, now leap a creek,
Now climb the rocky bluff; along the hill
They fly; make many a feint with cunning skill,

Nor leave the paper "scent" where dullest eye
May seek. Quick sight they ask, and feet that fly
Along the turf; enduring limb and wind,
And hearty boyhood's cheer : 'tis these that send
The hares o'er many a puzzling zigzag mile,
Like swallows' swiftest flight, o'er wall and stile.
They honor swift pursuit, and mighty dread
The peering eye, the fleetest foot, or head
That sounds their wiles, and sights them from the hill.
And then with bugle cheer heads off until
They near the hares. Alas! full oft I've led
The nimble feet along yon hills, and sped
Away to Newmarket town; full oft the wood
We've coursed in gallant, buoyant hardihood;
Full oft has thrilled, the rocky hills among,
Our merry cheer from schoolboy's jolly tongue;
Full oft, with merry song and shout, that town
Has echoed loud to embryos of the gown.
O Time! give back to me one little hour
Such as we've passed therein; suspend thy power

JOHN PHILLIPS.
The founder of Phillips Exeter Academy.

"*And Phillips' halls I know no more.*" (*page 90.*)

O'er waning youth. Oh, grant me but this boon!
I weep. Youth's fleeting wing hath flown too soon.
The healthful bands that yearly sought that town
Are scattered far and wide. Some wear the gown;
And some try Fortune's varying, fickle wheel;
Some tread Pacific's strand, there try their weal;
Old Europe's clime a few have sought; and one
Dear boy, my friend, my heart, in grief or fun,
My other half[1] — with you I've loved to be,
And cleave the azure billows bold and free.
With you I've breasted many a nightly tide;
Together we have sought the ocean's side;
Together roamed the wood, the tiresome book
Forsook, and sought some grove, some quiet nook.

[1] "Ah, te meæ si partem animæ rapit
 Maturior vis."

HORACE

"And the last, my other heart,
 And almost my half self."

TENNYSON: *Princess.*

And dost thou say, my love, that soon thou'lt be
One of our band, and not a memory?
Since last we met, thy spirit, like a strain
Of dying music, lingers round, though main,
And different climes, divide. Thy lot hast been
To stand where many olden heroes, men
Translated to the sphere of gods in death,
Have stood, to scent the orange-blossom's breath,
A Marathon to view, Thermopylæ
To muse upon, Parnassus' mount to see,
And tread the land, and breathe the air, the gods
Did love — alas, where now the bondsman plods!
To look on Troy, the Hellespont to view,
Walk classic ground, con Homer's page anew,
And sail upon Ægean's deepest blue.

Ah God! Does freedom's light burn brightly forth
Save once two thousand years? And is the north
The only clime where flames the sacred torch?
And doth it blaze within itself to scorch

Existent life in southern tropic climes?
Is it a tree that only fruits at times,
Then dies, or falls beneath the traitor's hand
That plucked and ate, then held the firing brand?
And who will answer? Rome gave forth her all
Whilst thriving on its fruit, nor dreamt of fall,
Till civil strife laid low the sacred tree.
And Athens' tale is but the same. The free,
The free! — "eternal vigilance is thy price."
Columbia's sons, to keep this boon, now twice
Have fought. And may this arm be nerved anew,
In youth or age, to serve our banner true,
Or fall beneath the red, the white, and blue!

I own no dinner poet's flattering muse;
But who, from candor's heart, can e'er refuse
To sing, e'en though it be a lowly strain
Of memories we ne'er may know again? —
Of friendship's ties too young to know deceit,
Of hallowed science in her green retreat,

Of mentor's sage instruction, father's care,
Who felt that boyhood's lot was once his share,
Forgave the wayward, knew that all may sin,
The truant taught where to again begin,
And with those deep-souled noble eyes did beam
Fit approbation on the dawning gleam
Of talent, but with terror awed the wag.
For thee sincere my love, though like a drag
Thy mathematic rules; thy clear-brained thought,
Howe'er I toiled, a maze it only brought.

And honest Cato, now my mind to thee
Instinctive turns, when memory like a sea
Doth roll its mighty waves upon the past;
And nought there seems, alas! to fade so fast
As those sweet joys we once could call our own, —
Those joys that each have had, how quickly flown!
Amid the storm my mind doth turn to yours
For sympathy and cheer: my heart assures

My wayward mind 'twill find a listening ear
In thy great soul that knows a feeling tear.
Thou ruledst with lenity our boisterous throng,
And graved thy love, nor ever did a wrong
Upon full many a young and tender heart.

When odorous spring breathes fresh from sunny vales,
When blooming flowers the beauteous scene regales,
When the lilac and the rose are sweetest to view,
Their perfumes are elysian, and the blue
Above doth wear its deepest, richest hue,
We plant the spreading elm upon this green.
Thou whispering elm, we leave thee and this scene.
'Twere vain; but yet in schoolboy pride we name
Thee Onward, chant in christening hymns thy fame,
And as thy leaves shall scatter in the blast
Each pensive autumn brings, so we at last
Must quit these scenes, be borne on fortune's gale,
How far apart! Each class that leaves this band,
Like billows fast succeeding on the strand,

Doth chant its funeral dirge, its last sad lay,
And quickly passes from our sight away.
Thou whispering elm, endeared to us alone,
Dodona's leafy shrine, in mystic tone
Communion sweet with gods and men did keep;
And canst thou, when the summer breezes sweep
Thy limbs, like harpstrings struck by fingers soft,
In ancient, mystic ways waft tidings oft?
When autumn's anthem, pensive, low, and sweet,
Doth kiss thy waving form, then canst thou greet
Some wayworn wanderer of our scattered throng
With tidings low and sweet, with pensive song?
And when thou'rt grown to be a mighty tree,
And chant the oriole sweet lullaby,
And softly rock him in his hanging nest,
When thou art in thy rising vigor blest,
Then wilt thou know the tottering limbs, perchance,
That falter to thy shade, as 'twere in trance,
To see thee grown so high, *then* wilt thou know
The silvered heads, the boys of years ago?

SCHOOLDAYS.

As two fond lovers on a foreign shore
Await in sorrow's throes, and both implore
That tireless Time may hold his flight, nor grant
The hour when he must rend the bonds, implant
In love's sweet soil a thorn it ne'er hast known,—
Await in grief the hour, their joys all flown,
When he, alas! must cross the stormy main,
And she, in accents wild, or speechless pain,
Implores him not to go, and rend for aye
His cherished form, and make of love's bright day
Chill sorrow's night: so we by destiny
Are hurried on. Our hearts in buoyancy
Would gladly linger on this sweetest scene,
Nor tempt the billowy sea of time unseen.

Long may ye stand, ye noble, beauteous walls!
Long may old Time look kindly on these halls!
Long may the rising sun thy gilded spire
Light up, and feel his warmest evening fire!

SCHOOLDAYS.

Long may the locust-trees sweet fragrance breathe
Around these quiet walls, the youth beneath
Their shade disport upon this ancient green!
Long may the balm-of-gileads wave between
Thy cloistered, classic halls, and heaven on high!
Long may these wide-spread elms thy beauty grace,
And add perfection to thy lovely face!
Long may thy clock ring out the passing hour,
And tell the boys life's cares upon them lower;
That rosy youth will soon, too soon, be o'er;
That fleeting time looks backward nevermore!

    Ring wild and free, old iron bell;
        Ring glad and joyously!
    Your dying century ring, old bell;
        Ring, bell, ring glad and free!

    Ring o'er this classic scene, old bell;
        Ring glad and joyously!
    Ring out, old bell, thy dying knell,
        Thy waning century!

The swiftly passing hours ring, bell;
    Ring glad and joyously!
The youth, from clear-toned lips, you tell,
    Be merry, happy, free!

And on the moonlight's silver air
    Ring glad and joyously!
And when the rising stars are fair,
    Ring, bell, ring bold and free!

And to the spangled wintry sky
    Ring glad and joyously!
And to thy gentle stream near by
    Ring out thy minstrelsy!

Ring wild and free, old iron bell;
    Ring glad and joyously!
Your dying century ring, old bell;
    Ring, bell, ring glad and free!

MISCELLANEOUS.

A VISION.

> "I would recall a vision which I dreamed,
> Perchance in sleep; for in itself a thought,
> A slumbering thought, is capable of years,
> And curdles a long life into one hour."
>
> BYRON.

I HAD a vision. O'er me softly swept
The tide of memory; and down the vale
Of childhood's years, before me stood a boy.
His mien was grave beyond his early years;
His locks of flowing light the wind caressed.
He stood beside a gently-flowing stream,
And wept; his youthful heart was wrung with grief.
And in the little vale coursed by that stream,
With groves of richest growth upon the right,
And a long hill with woods upon the left,

The summer sun was sinking in the west.
Beside its molten orb a hamlet stood,
And on its spires he shed his dying ray.
There stood a cottage in that nestled fold,
And on a couch therein there lay a form
That oft by night in dreams before him stood.
Her angel beauty, eyes of languid hue,
Foretold that immortality was near.
As twilight came he stood with eyes upturned
To where the evening star first twinkling shone.
He knew not why, but yet he gazed thereon
Full long, then looked to where the hamlet stood,
And wept full sore. His o'erwrought nature slept.

Now, while he slept, her spirit angels bore
On pinions soft unto that silver star.

My vision changed. I saw the people throng
With slow and reverent tread the village church.

A VISION.

The old and young, the high and low, were there;
And in that throng there stood the boy alone.
Amid a sorrowing people, sore he wept.
His heart was full, that it did nearly break.
The sorrowing people bore her to the grave:
But he went not; he homeward turned his way
In silent, heavy sadness, void of thought,
That baffles sympathy and sweet repose.

Now, time sped on: the lilies sprung above
Her grave, and immortality's emblem grew
Above her lowly sleep.
      The vision changed.
'Twas sabbath eve. There stood beside that grave
A tall and comely youth in pensive mood;
And in the holy stillness of that scene
He fain would kneel, and ask a benison
Upon that cherished dust. A flower from
That grave he bore, and locked it in his heart.

A VISION.

The vision changed. Upon the stormy wave
Of human life I saw a youthful form;
And with that storm he battled brave and long,
And distant, homeless climes he travelled o'er,
And learning's golden lore he eager sought.

My vision changed. With pale and haggard look,
From toil and sorrow, midnight's sapping page,
I saw him homeward turn his saddened way;
And none did greet him at his former home,
And none did know him at the hamlet's inn.
He turned him to the little burial-place.
'Twas winter: yet that emblem flower throve,
Of immortality; and he did pluck
A leaf, and place it in his bosom's fold,
And there, reflecting on the war of life
That he had fruitless waged, he bitter wept.
Yet, from the hallowed spell the grave doth bring,
Sweet consolation o'er him spread her wings;

And he did leave that little burial-place
In sweeter, holier mood than he had felt
Since years, long years, had sped their course away.

NOTE. — The reader will at once see that the versification of this poem is similar to that of Byron's entitled "The Dream." Though clad in the garb of that most beautiful poem, the subject is the author's.

EDITH.

> "That thou hast been to me all tenderness,
> And friend to more than human friendship just."
>
> CAMPBELL.

I HAD a vision fair. A stream beside
   Of broad yet gentle flow, a youth and maid
Did stand, and pensive watch it onward glide.
   Upon its face the dying sunbeams played;
Far stretching southward lay the hoary main,
Where waters everlasting marked their reign.

They stood upon a ruined fortress old,
   Where freedom's fearless gathered yoemen fought
And bled and died,— oh, nobly fought! where gold,
   And balked ambition, pride, did offer nought
But terms of craven death. His neighbor's blood,
By Arnold's hand here mingled with the flood.

EDITH.

Yon granite towering shaft through ages long
   Thy ignominy, crime, base man, shall tell;
And Arnold, traitor's name, be wove in song
   As he who willed our freedom's cause to sell.
A mighty people execrate thy name,
And every schoolboy read thy road to shame.

The dead, their sons among, sleep peaceful here.
   The scene is rural now; no gathering din
Of war is heard; there drops no widowed tear;
   No father, brother, husband, here begin
The harvest reaped by Death; the grazing kine
Roam o'er this scene, above its powder-mine.

The early eve drew on; the stars came out;
   The river's darkly-heaving breast was set
With lambent jewels from on high; without
   The river's mouth, where stream and ocean met,
An hundred sails were riding, strongly chained:
So calm the sea, not one its cable strained.

The dews like richest incense filled the air;
  The latest swallow twittering whirled on high;
Unto their folds the flocks did make repair;
  The cottage smoke wreathed upward to the sky;
The night-hawk sang the dirge of dying day,
While distant rang the sailor's roundelay.

And to and fro, like Charon's spirit bark,
  The village shallops glided o'er that stream;
And sloops with wizard sails adown the dark
  And swollen tide did float; the latest gleam
Of day was fading fast; the fisher's eye
Peered through the dark his cottage to descry.

But hark! the youth, till now so deaf to all
  Save Edith's accents sweet, doth catch a sound.
He lists; his neighing steeds unto him call.
  He hears their hoofs impatient paw the ground;
They fret to give his carriage fleetest wing,
And from their steel-clad hoofs the gravel fling.

She mutely lay within his fond embrace;
  Her raven locks dishevelled downward hung.
O God! if heavenly bliss within this space
  To mortals given there be, 'tis love when young:
It is the new-born spirit's waking love,
A lamb in meekness; innocence, the dove.

O Edith! must I leave this fondest scene?
  O God! my brain doth reel, my heart is gone,
To think of thee, my love, and memories green!
  O Edith! press thy sweetest lips upon
My fevered ones; again, and once again!
And must we part, again to meet, ah! when?

LOVED ISLE.

Loved isle begirt with ocean's foam,
    Adieu! I go athwart the sea;
But long thy form, where'er I roam,
    Shall rest impressed on memory, —

Thy rugged rocks, thy moss-hung trees,
    The spruce, the fir, the ash, that grow,
And break the storm, yet fan the breeze,
    And clothe thy hills above, below; —

Where cranes and ravens nightly perch,
    And fleecy flocks seek feed below,
Among thy rugged, gnarly birch,
    Where sea-gulls flutter to and fro.

Adieu, thou lone and rugged isle,
  A rugged people's seagirt home;
Thou lonely home, adieu, a while!
  'Tis fate that bids me onward roam.

REMEMBRANCE.

> "Thought would destroy their paradise.
> No more: where ignorance is bliss,
> 'Tis folly to be wise."
>
> GRAY.

AND can it be that youth has flown,
   That rosy, fleeting youth is o'er,
That manhood sternly claims his own,
   And Phillips' halls I know no more?

And can it be no more I tread
   Again those vine-clad, classic halls;
That boyhood's hours have quickly fled,
   And I a stranger to those walls?

And can it be those elm-hung streets,
   And Phillips' ever cherished green,

This day another throng now greets,
  And we forgotten on that scene?

And can it be I walk no more
  The Eddy's sacred, cool retreat;
Nor Exeter, with fern-fringed shore,
  Where oft I've fled the summer's heat?

No more I hear thy whispering pine,
  Sweet stream, nor rowlocks' hoarse reply:
Ah! ne'er again they will be mine,
  Save on the page of memory.

No more upon thy placid wave
  In listless mood I downward float;
No more therein these limbs I lave,
  And hear the partridge drum his note.

No more on Squamscot's heaving tide
  In idleness we downward float;

No more we swim his current wide,
   Nor listen to the boatman's note.

In joyful mood another band
   Again will course each winding street,
Nor think, alas! a foreign land
   Owns one who sighs o'er memories sweet.

Anew each rural, fond retreat
   With boyish pride and zeal explore,
In blessed ignorance repeat -
   The games, the songs we've sung before.

The ocean's low and distant moan,
   As heard full oft on Bunker Hill,
Has lost the solemn, deep-mouthed tone
   That made my schoolboy heart to thrill.

Within those classic halls, beyond
   The boundless, heaving ocean's breast,

REMEMBRANCE.

This day is heard the footsteps' sound
   Of more — and we a tale at best.

My midnight lamp another's page
   Now lights within my cloistered cell;
While I upon life's pilgrimage
   Have journeyed long where strangers dwell.

Oh, these, all these, I know no more!
   I only feel, too deeply feel,
That youthful joys, alas! are o'er,
   And nought this heart-sickness can heal.

O Time! give back those days of yore,
   With each secluded rural scene,
Upon my native distant shore,
   Where memories will long be green.

O Time! give back those hours of joy
   That gild with gold fond memory's sky,

When each was nothing but a boy,
　　And school-days never knew a sigh.

O God! it breaks my heaving heart,
　　As now I backward look on thee,
Sweet scene, and we so far apart,
　　To know thou'rt lost for aye to me.

———•———

A REPLY.

"But Codrus was a poet,
　　And all the townfolks know it;
None other pens such lines
The human heart defines
　　With master skill,
　　With master skill."

A REPLY.

"Your paper now can boast
Nought but our poet's ghost;
And all are sickly lines,
Round which his shadow twines,
  To give them life,
  To give them life."

But, John, I'll pit the nation
Against your conversation,
That labors on and on,
While hearers yawn and yawn:
  You've ta'en too much,
  You've ta'en too much.

For Codrus *still* doth write
Those lines you call so trite,
Such paltry schoolboy stuff,
In measures rude and rough,
  That has no thought,
  That has no thought.

A REPLY.

The trouble is, your pate,
Where partial judgment sate,
And bigotry most foul
Doth thrive, and feed, and growl,
    Is fogged with wine,
    Is fogged with wine.

MARY.

"Through the blue deep thou wingest."
SHELLEY.

AND my love has left me,
   And my heart is sad,
And it has bereft me:
   Would that I were dead!

And the bells ring dreary,
   And the night is dark;
And I drift a-weary
   In my lonely bark.

And that star above me,
   And its silver beam,
And her heart that loves me,
   Call me o'er life's stream.

And my heart's deep longing
And her calling hand
Are no earth's belonging,
But of spirit land.

CREW SONG.

SWIFTLY glides our gallant crew,
Strong of bone and tough sinew,
Down the winding Charles,
Down the winding Charles!

Sweat is on each manly brow:
Like an arrow flies our prow
O'er the waters blue,
O'er the waters blue.

How each blade the water ploughs!
How the strokes our blood arouse,
Sweeping on, darting on,
Sweeping on, darting on!

Onward, onward, now we glide
O'er the river's heaving tide,
   Keeping time, beating time,
   To our oar-blades' merry rhyme.

GATHERING FAGOTS.

CHILDREN are here from the wood:
   Poverty's children are they,
Bringing for many a rood,
   Bringing with toil all the way,
Stowing behind in the garth,
Fagots to feed the lone hearth.

Chilling the winds are now here,
   Breathing from out the cold vale;
Night-time is hastening near,
   Wasting their visages pale.
Homeward they wearily go,
Chilled by the wind and the snow.

Squamscot with banks that are lined,
   Crowned with the wealth of the year,
Asks as it leaves them behind,
   Pleads with the rich that are here,
All through the wintery hour,
Care for the child of the poor.

MY LOVE.

THRICE welcome guest, my love, this morn:
    These hours of sadness that hang round,
And shroud each day with robes of thorn,
    Thy presence hurls upon the ground.

With thee to be, commune by night
    Alone with thee, has been my joy;
In loneliness with thee, how bright
    The world of woe! no pangs annoy.

I love thy presence by the stream
    When all is still save Nature's voice,
When nought intrudes, when silvered beams
    Of midnight's moon my soul rejoice.

Thy presence by the lake's clear sheen,
Thy holy impulse in the mount,
Thy mighty awe, thy sombre mien
Where ocean rolls, my joy doth count.

HARVEST FESTIVAL.

> "Dulce periculum est,
> O Lenae, sequi deum."
>
> HORACE.

WHEN fields are shorn, and mows are filled,
    'Tis meet to gather round
The harvest-feast, put off all cares,
    And shut out labor's sound.

Before the rowen needs the scythe,
    And cider-presses call
The farmer to his task, 'tis fit
    To feast, both one and all.

Just as the pear with mellow cheek
    Vies with the barley's yellow,

And melons great and rich are ripe,
'Tis good to get right mellow.

When nuts are falling, — hazel, all,
From beech to great walnut, —
And early leaves have strewed the ground,
'Tis right — get drunk — all but.

MY ANGEL SLEEPS.

> "Our life is twofold: sleep hath its own world,
> A boundary between the things misnamed
> Death and existence."
> BYRON.

MY angel sleeps, and doth not hear
   Her lover's softly whispering call.
The spirit wafts around and near
   Its nightly flight, beyond the pall
We blindly name mortality.
   The flesh, the spirit's casket, lies
Inwrapped in sleep mysteriously.
   Nor could her spirit's mystic ties
With that we slumber call commune,
   Were I to press these burning lips
To hers, and slake my heart; but soon
   Will spirit that now flits and skips,

Released from burdening transient clay,
　Take on its mortal guise, and beam
Its love on me. I thought delay
　To clasp in fond embrace did seem
To starve my yearning, burning love;
　But let her wearied form repose.

'TIS SWEET.

'TIS sweet to hear the voice of one
    We love, a friend, or cherished tone
Of her that's more to us alone
    Than all the world beside.

'Tis sweet to hear the welcome call
Of him who's been our stay, or all;
Yet sweetly sad doth ever fall
    His parting, fond adieu.

'Tis pleasant, as we stroll along
The bank of childhood's brook, among
The scenes that call in memory's throng;
    But ah, how sad to leave!

'TIS SWEET.

We love to hear the swelling strain
Of music as it falls, again
To rise on evening's glad refrain;
  But sweetly sad's the dying sound.

'Tis sweet to dream of childhood's scenes,
Again to walk adown the green
And lovely vale our youth has seen:
  We can't believe we're old.

On, on, we dream, in fond deceit,
Nor once e'er think it's childhood's cheat,
Till oh, the dream with dainty feet
  Has fled, and we awake, how sad!

LONGING.

AND shall my love forever be
    Unfed? And shall the cursèd ties
Of sin we call society
    Restrain this passion of the skies?

I saw her pass with angel grace:
    My lovesick eyes did look and turn;
For halo sat upon that face,
    As if mortality to spurn.

And I did love, as oft before;
    But ah! too fiercely flamed the fire
Within the torch I madly bore
    On to my passion's funeral pyre.

Yet, Venus like, though often chilled,
　My love forever shall remain;
Flame on, flame on, nor e'er be skilled
　With guile to forge the tempter's chain.

O heavenly flame! O child of light!
　This sinful world were paradise,
If thou didst always reign in might,
　Nor veil thyself within the skies.

EPIGRAM.

WHEN gray-haired men of fifty-five
    Pair off with maids of twenty,
God bless their souls! and may they thrive;
But *men* should be more plenty.